How to have

THE AWESOME POWER OF PUBLIC SPEAKING

Peter J Daniels

OTHER TITLES BY PETER J. DANIELS
How To Be Happy Though Rich
How To Reach Your Life Goals
How To Handle A Major Crisis
How To Be Motivated All The Time

How To Have The Awesome Power Of Public Speaking
Copyright © 1988 by Peter J. Daniels
National Library of Australia card number
and ISBN 0 949330 25 6

The author would like to thank Geoff Strelan for his valued
assistance in the writing of this book.

Cover Photo: Gregory Steer, Adelaide.

Printed by Griffin Press Limited
262 Marion Road, Netley.
South Australia.

Published by **The House of Tabor**
  84 Northgate Street,
  Unley Park, South Australia 5061.

in co-operation with
Peter J. Daniels Business & Investment Consultants,
155 Waymouth Street,
Adelaide, South Australia 5000.

If I speak in the tongues
of angels, but have not love,
I am only a clanging cymbal.
(1 Corinthians 13:1 NIV)

Dedicated to my wife, Robina, who recognised before anyone else that God could use my words to change lives for good.

Speaking in public is the ultimate art form, without music, props, or extra players. You are all alone — to win or lose.

The direct relationship between speaker and crowd allows only for truth in delivery and reception. It emphasises the slightest flaw and aggravates the most minute disturbance. What is said cannot be unsaid, what has failed cannot be resurrected and what has been good or acceptable can be destroyed by the next breath.

Contents

Preface

At 26 years of age, I was a bricklayer, with very limited education and pretty fuzzy comprehension. Yet within my soul was a desperate, urgent, compelling desire to communicate. I did not at this stage have any message — only a feeling that I had something burning inside that had to get out; and I was prepared to trade my life for it.

The trigger that exploded my life into what I was to become (and am still becoming) was released on May 25th, 1959, at a Billy Graham crusade. It was to take me on an endless journey around the world, into the offices of presidents, film stars and celebrities of all kinds, into the dizzy world of high finance and, by contrast, to the corners of the earth in war zones where poverty and depravation of the worst possible kind prevailed.

I never looked back, because I was changed; I was different and it was permanent. I had experienced something akin to Wesley when 'his heart was strangely warmed,' or, as others have put it, I was 'exposed with clarity to a moment of truth'.

I have often tried to explain it to my wife and family: I hear a different song or music that is beyond description but ever present. With its magic rhythm, it sets the direction for my journey, like the Pied Piper of Hamlyn. The sound goes on — sometimes quickening the pace, sometimes more slowly, but always with the same haunting call to obey.

In those early days, I was asked to speak at a Sunday School anniversary for 25 minutes. I was a miserable failure and spoke, haltingly and in a state of fear, for about eight minutes — and then folded speechless and full of despair. When I got home, I wept. I had thought that my compelling desire to speak would be enough, but the result was nothing but empty platitudes without structure or theme.

Having recovered somewhat, I enrolled in a Public Speaking class to try and learn the techniques that would help me fulfil my dream. As I sat and listened to the instructor, my heart sank and I walked out, never to return again. The lecturer's own ability to speak in public was inadequate. I knew that I needed to rise above the mediocrity of that teacher, and I was afraid that if I stayed in the course, I might get locked into a style and presence that would never become awesome or great.

I went home and read what Abraham Lincoln had said: 'I will study and prepare and my opportunity will come.' For the next five years, almost every day, I polished my diction and dialogue, listening to my speeches on a tape recorder and correcting what I thought were obvious flaws.

During that time, although involved in many areas of church and social work, I was given little opportunity to speak in public. On one rare occasion, I was asked to preach at our church. I received a tremendous response from the congregation — only to have the pastor say, 'You must have copied that from someone else.' I was never invited to preach again!

It was at this time that my wife, Robina, recognised that I had something different, and that somehow I had what was to be described by others a long time later as 'the awesome power of public speaking'.

And so, with openness and affection to all who have heard a different sound and want to express it to others, I take you through the well learned lessons of the past 30 years — my pilgrimage to *the awesome power of public speaking.*

CHAPTER ONE

A Special Communication

To share with one person your thoughts, challenges and dreams is a unique personal relationship; but to transfer that same message to thousands, or even millions, with acceptance is a great and awesome privilege available only to a few.

CHAPTER ONE

A Special Communication

If you have the privilege of speaking to a group, large or small, you need to understand the very special relationship involved.

You stand alone with your ability, open for all to observe; there is no chance of retraction or change, and all mistakes, omissions and flaws become like giant pincers taking off big chunks of your confidence and presence of mind, leaving you more vulnerable and fractured each time.

It *is* lonely standing on an empty stage with spotlights, real or imagined, focused on you, and 10 to 10,000 faces glued to your every sound and movement, riveting your consciousness with the incalculable awareness that you have nothing to help, protect or defend you except your finely tuned ability to create the mood and win the day.

Your focus must always be carefully aimed at your audience. Understand that they are vulnerable against the awesome, practised power of speech. If in your opening words you asked the audience to stand, they would. For that matter, they would do anything within reason.

So the crowd is vulnerable to you in the sense that they are prepared, at the beginning at least, to do what you say. You have the strength of the relationship in your hands.

You always have before you a voluntary audience. All crowds, large or small, can react to a speaker, even if they are in a confined setting. I have watched audiences in prisons, schools, military and business situations where theoretically the speaker was the actual power holder, or was given the power by virtue of some authority. But coughing, yawning and physical movements proved yet again that all audiences are voluntary listeners. All speakers need to recognise that no matter what external authority they have, public speaking is a definite two way street with certain rules and etiquette to be observed.

The fact that an audience is usually sitting gives a psychological advantage to the speaker, because sitting is a posture of submission. Even when an audience is standing, the attitude is submissive. They are waiting for each one of your words, which results in a hearing submission which is another component in this very special communication relationship.

So there you are all alone, quite vulnerable. But so is the audience who have volunteered to hear you. They are in a submissive frame of mind, ready to move into the next category of behaviour, which is an eager or critical anticipation.

You see the trust or critical anticipation in their eyes or their body posture, and sense the mood of the crowd by some intuitive ability that is difficult to describe. It is at this very sensitive time that you can change or adopt a mood according to the direction required. If you do not set a predetermined course at this juncture, then you will find it difficult later and may even lose your advantage and be swayed by the crowd. That could lead you to lose direction and become submissive or apologetic in your presentation.

A delicate balance between the speaker and the audience is maintained by understanding that you are in a situation where there is little or no direct verbal response, unless you have scope for questions or you use a deliberate, provocative 'response-getter'. Unless you are in a very unusual environment which has been created beforehand or, for some reason, you have to justify your position, then there is generally a sense of anticipation and acceptance of what you are about to say.

This special communication has within its boundaries very little by way of restriction, but enormous possibilities for creativity and response. To take this lightly can result in embarrassment, ridicule and even anger because an audience will not long tolerate frivolous, careless and impertinent behaviour directed towards them.

The safest way to deal with any public speaking opportunity is to combine integrity and intelligence with an attitude of gratitude to those who are prepared to open their minds and hearts to your thoughts. Those who wait for your words are fellow-travellers in life and desire from you the warmth and friendship you would demonstrate toward a dear friend. In fact, your future friends will probably be drawn from such a group as this.

To share with one person your thoughts, challenges and dreams is a unique personal relationship; but to transfer that same message to thousands, or even millions, with acceptance is a great and awesome privilege available only to a few.

Meditate on this very special communication often, because as you realise the depth of this rare opportunity and relationship, you will become more sensitive to its uniqueness and thereby continually improve your performance.

PRINCIPLES
1. The public speaker is very alone.
2. The audience is vulnerable.
3. The audience is present voluntarily.
4. The audience is in a submissive posture.
5. At the beginning there is eager or critical anticipation.
6. Public speaking involves little direct verbal response.
7. Public speaking is a special privilege.

CHAPTER TWO

Know Your Message

From the moment you are introduced as the speaker until the time you leave the podium the extent of your preparation will be quite clearly revealed.

Know Your Message

It is amazing how many speakers have so little to say. It's not that their time on the platform is too short or that they demonstrate an inability to use a great number of words! I am thinking of the numbing of the crowd by a repetitious, bland, unstructured conglomeration of words which leaves the listener wondering what it was all about.

In every public communication there needs to be a specific message or theme which can be reduced to no more than two or three lines. Keep refining the theme of your message until it could be clearly understood if you said it by telegram. Then, and only then, should you prepare the 'how to' and 'why' which covers the full scope of what is to be said.

The next essential is a total commitment to your theme. When you have a desperate desire to persuade your audience, that urgent commitment to your message will release the awesome power that elevates what you have to say above mediocrity.

In preparation for your message, research must be done to ensure that your claim is securely built on fact. It is at these times that your reading habits will prove to be permanently useful because the vocabulary of your reading, according to its breadth and frequency, will come to your aid. Since 1950 there has been an explosion of information available and it seems to me that those who want to be reasonably informed would have to read a minimum of two books a week, carefully selected and directed to your life's goals. I underline my books where information is pertinent and then get those areas typed out and put into a composite book which could have up to 50 titles. At any given time I can relate to those 50 composite books within a very short time.

Preparation should be a lifetime commitment but specific preparation is an absolute necessity if you are to develop the awesome power of public speaking. From the moment you are introduced as the speaker until the time you leave the podium the extent of your preparation will be quite clearly revealed.

In preparing for that important speech you must know much more about your subject than what you actually say, and details reflecting the thoroughness of your study will bring an obvious confidence to your manner and tone.

It is also important to have clearly defined boundaries for your talk. In most cases it is impossible to handle all aspects of any subject. So you must keep your talk within boundaries that will indicate that you have covered the basic elements but your audience can ask you to come back to give more information.

To endeavour to cover all aspects of a subject in one speaking appointment will garble your message and confuse your audience. As well, you miss out on emphasis, dramatics, modulation and many other essential ingredients of a successful talk.

When you have prepared by research, attention must then be given to refining the subject matter down to the essentials. This filtering process, like the condensed stories in *The Reader's Digest,* must maintain the flow of information without encumbering the listener with unnecessary packaging.

Because of the depth of your preparation and your commitment you can be sure that you not only know the road ahead but you can safely travel on it. Many times after a speech the speaker is stunned to hear the Master of Ceremonies announce, without consultation, that a time for questions is available. I have often heard a speaker give a splendid address, and then at question time some obscure person in the audience who has some knowledge of the subject asks a question that throws the speaker's supposed knowledge out of the window because his answer was either not relevant or accurate or even sensible.

Prepare, prepare, prepare, so that you have confidence about the road ahead and can cap off any speech with 'I told you so', and so confirm your value and authority as the chosen speaker.

PRINCIPLES
1. You must have an overall theme.
2. You must have a desperate desire to persuade.
3. Preparation ensures power.
4. You must know more than you say.
5. All facts must be filtered to essentials.
6. You must know the way ahead.

CHAPTER THREE

Set the Scene

In a sense all public speakers are performers and therefore have entertainment value. On that basis, staging, dress and technical details are important.

CHAPTER THREE

Set the Scene

I had been travelling for 38 hours from Australia to a destination in the U.S.A. There were delays caused by engine problems and bad weather and I only had time for a shower, shave and a cup of coffee before I went into an all day international board meeting. After the meeting I was fortunate to have enough time for a 20 minute soak in a hot bath and 30 minutes sleep before I had to get dressed again and deliver a three and a half hour evening seminar to a very large, astute, professional, audience.

At other times I have been in areas where there were revolutions, riots, and all kinds of delays and discomforts which are part and parcel of every day life. Once I was in hospital with an antibiotic drip, but 30 minutes before I was to speak I had the tubes removed, got dressed, left hospital and went on stage. If the audience had not been told by the Master of Ceremonies, I doubt whether anyone would have guessed what condition I was in.

The reason I am sharing this with you is that there are many, many other imaginable and un-imaginable things that can happen to professional public speakers from time to time, but they must never change your attitude or performance.

When you hit the platform you must bounce, and anything other than a 100% performance should give you shame. Your visual form must always suggest confidence and dignity, and you must never behave any other way irrespective of fears, nerves, sickness or tiredness. Never adver-tise your difficulties.

A professional speaker must be alert, look alert and stay alert at all times before, during and after a performance. If at any time you cannot do that and give of your ultimate best then do not under any circumstance be seen or heard in public.

One of the most unsettling things for a public speaker is the silent hall or room. It creates a mood all of its own that intimidates both the speaker and the audience. Silence by itself indicates nothing-ness and is the opposite of what public speaking is all about. Creating a special mood cannot be done in silence except on the most solemn and sombre occasions.

I always suggest a background of music which complements the theme and the nature of the presentation. Obviously it would be unwise to have stirring marching music for a speaker who is going to discuss art — a fine orchestral presentation of the classics would be far more suitable. For a motivational speaker the theme of 'Rocky' would be most appropriate. So the music tends to create the mood you require.

Music is also important at the conclusion because it allows the audience to stop and think rather than feel obliged to involve themselves in conversation with someone next to them, which they may not feel disposed to do at that moment.

If you can, avoid sitting on the stage by yourself or with others during commencement proceedings, as this can be very unsettling. The heat of spotlights, the effect of stage lighting on your eyes or the incredible draughts that so often find their way through the corridors backstage and then escape through the stage outlet, disrupting your notes and hair — all these make you feel worse than you ought to be. At the same time your presence on the stage removes a sense of anticipation from your audience. If the preliminaries are long, you are prevented from adjusting your speech, attending to toilet, or having a drink or a throat lozenge.

Technical preparation is also essential. It may seem obvious, but the first step here is to check the sound system. Avoid arriving just in time to speak. Very often the sound system will not be to your liking. Sometimes you will even have to stop at the beginning of your talk for adjustment and echo removal. Check all sound systems and electrical equipment *before* the function begins, particularly making sure that the light on the speaker's podium works and is adequate and that overhead lighting is not nullified by a spotlight.

If you are in an overseas country and the language is different, go over your notes with your interpreter and make sure he or she understands not only the individual words and phrases but also the *meaning*. Test thoroughly the serious aspects to ensure full understanding.

It always pays to have a few local people in attendance when you practice. Watch their faces as you make points and observe a response or otherwise. Do not be satisfied with a 'quick fix' because anything in another language must be done with great sensitivity and care.

Even your own language can vary greatly in its meaning from country to country. For example, in many areas of the United States of America to 'table a certain item or subject' at a board meeting means to dismiss or remove that item; but in Australia it has the opposite meaning — you open it up for discussion and allow total participation by all in attendance. So seek out and learn something about the local customs and idioms to enable you to speak with awesome power and not make a stupid mistake somewhere along the way that nullifies all you have said.

Most speakers pay very little attention to dress. Yet if we look at the real crowd pleasers and movers it is the razzle dazzle that gives the entertainer, who is the object of all eyes and ears, additional credibility.

In a different way, if you want to speak in public with awesome power, attention must be given to staging and dress. I am not suggesting costume or flashy lights, but I am suggesting an approach that fits the occasion. For instance, if you were going to speak on success you would not go onto the platform unshaven, with uncut hair, old denim jeans, torn shirt and open sandles with long dirty toenails poking through. As ridiculous as this sounds, I have seen speakers so badly dressed and groomed they have put themselves behind scratch just by their appearance.

Pay particular attention to your offstage image, particularly with photographs, and learn the simple but important techniques of being photographed right. It was years before a photographer in the United States told me to drop my chin and look squarely at the camera for my best results. The difference is outstanding. Learn something about posture, etiquette, photography and dress. To assist in those areas you need help — take advice from experts.

The truth is you never get a second chance on a first impression. While there may be some who feel that clothes do not make the man or woman, no one would argue with the fact that the way one is dressed acts as an introduction. I have always found that a dark suit with white contrasting shirt or blouse gives the impression that you are serious about your work and you've dressed to compliment your audience.

Staging is an important component as well. I see many instances where the speaker's podium is at one side of the stage, but I believe that it robs the speaker of contact with the whole audience and disadvantages the audience who are on the wrong side of the stage.

I avoid moving down to and through the audience while speaking for the obvious reason that although it puts you closer to some people, it has four major setbacks.

1. It removes you from your place of power and reference (i.e. if you have a mental blank you are without your reference notes).
2. It removes you from the powerful position of eye contact with a large number of your audience.
3. It puts you right in front of some people, but others see only your back and feel somewhat distant and alienated from you.
4. Your sound system may go haywire because there are usually other microphones or amplifiers around the hall and at the most crucial moment it could all go crazy.

Be extremely careful of the magnified noise of

shuffling papers by the microphone or directing the audience to something on their program or notes that disturbs the whole atmosphere and distracts attention from your talk.

In a sense all public speakers are performers and therefore have entertainment value. On that basis, staging, dress and technical details are important. It's part of your preparation.

PRINCIPLES
1. Never advertise your difficulties.
2. Beware of the silent hall.
3. Avoid being on stage at commencement.
4. Check electrical equipment.
5. Dress is part of your preparation.
6. Staging affects communication.
7. Avoid moving down to the audience.

Get the Tone Right

Always try to use a controlled tone which gives the impression that you have a great deal more power under the bonnet than you are using.

CHAPTER FOUR

Get the Tone Right

One of my greatest helps as I began to train myself in public speaking was a tape recorder. I am more than a little embarrassed by those early efforts as I listen to my nasal tones and my high pitched voice, which irritated me every time I forced myself to listen to my clumsy performance and my static style.

I suggest you tape every speech you make before you give it publicly. Iron out the wrinkles and persevere with the sound of your voice, aiming to develop expression and a tone that sounds warm and confident to the ears of others.

Examples of good tone can be experienced by listening to good radio and television news readers. Tone clarity and diction are of paramount importance. As well, consider the comments of friends and seek their opinions in respect to the sound of your voice, challenging them to be honest with you. Flattery will not help you at this point, but honest opinion will, because your friends represent the broad cross-section of people you will be aiming at in your audience.

When seeking to get a tone that suits your voice and style, be very careful not to develop a monotone delivery. Use modulation, not only in the sound of your voice, but also in your speed and diction by presenting some words and phrases slowly and deliberately and others fast and with machine gun rapidity.

Modulation will keep your speech more pleasant to the ear and, if directed properly, help to emphasise principles and points you have selected for special attention.

Never shout when speaking in public. You may have to raise your voice from time to time, and even become quite loud, but shouting takes the dignity out of your style and reminds your audience of mobs, agitators and street demonstrators. It has no place in the style of the professional speaker.

Dramatics must be used with perfect timing. Trying to dramatise too much takes the edge off your presentation and makes your message rather frivolous. It smacks of amateurism. But when used correctly, it is profoundly powerful. If you listen to the wartime speeches of Sir Winston Churchill, you will discover the awesome power it possessed. Churchill was probably more effective than anyone before or since as he mobilised the

English language and sent it into battle on behalf of a nation in great peril.

Be very careful not to use dramatics in the early part of your speech. Give the audience an opportunity to settle down; assess their mood as you prepare to create the atmosphere that *you* want for the occasion.

In any speech emotion must be used with great care because of its inherent ability to make one look and sound ridiculous or insincere, no matter how genuine or appropriate it may be.

I know a particular speaker who often cries when he speaks. It is not that he is insincere or that what he is referring to does not warrant a serious and sympathetic approach. An audience may want to express themselves through tears, but they feel they are eavesdropping on someone else's emotion when they see a speaker crying. It is very often embarrassing and uncomfortable. In fact, I have overheard members of an audience jokingly remark about the speaker's ability to switch tears on and off at will. It seems it is rarely appreciated or accepted as good communication.

The best way for a public speaker to show emotion is in word form. Give a solemn or robust word picture of the emotion to be expressed, in direct and accurate terms.

Remember to act out your role by your posture and body movements, which may range from slight to extravagant, according to the statements made. For instance, if you make a statement of action, then a clenched fist can be thrust forward; but if you are disclaiming or showing an abhorrence for something, then the palms of your hands can be put up. It is important to act out your role with body, hand and foot movements; even the use of your head is permissible and acceptable if it is done with good taste and a special dignity to suit the occasion.

Another example. It would be humorous and quite out of place for a speaker who was addressing a crowd on 'relaxation' to continually march and stomp around the platform, shouting to get the message across. By contrast, it would be ridiculous for a motivational speaker to be perfectly still, monotone and expressionless in delivering his message of action.

In acting out your role, however funny a situation is or whatever joke you tell, even if it is explosive, never, ever break into a laugh. It will not only unbalance your posture but could make you look quite ridiculous. As such emotions are exaggerated on stage you may even lose points.

Observe great comedians like Bob Hope present a most explosive joke. He just stands with a smile on his face which tends to add to the delight of his audience rather than raise the doubt that creeps into an audience's mind when you laugh at your own jokes. Smile when you deliver a joke, but never laugh.

Exceptional care must be taken with joke tell-ing. It takes a lot to recover from a joke that falls flat. Incredible practice in timing and tone must be done.

All jokes told by a public speaker must

1. be as original as possible,
2. have only one conclusion, and
3. be explosive in response.

If you cannot follow through that pattern then it might be wiser not to use the joke.

Always be on guard against careless and off-handed remarks which, when heard and head-lined, can minimise or even destroy your invol-vement for years. Occasionally we hear of the speaker who thought the microphone was turned off and made a very silly remark which was heard by all. *Ad-libbing* is an art possessed by very few speakers and should be avoided at all costs because the damage from unprepared remarks is difficult to repair.

Always try to use a controlled tone which gives the impression that you have a great deal more power under the bonnet than you are using. A controlled voice is like having a 10,000 horse power jet engine but using only half power — the sound indicates quite clearly you are having diffi-culty holding back the other 5,000 horse power but it could be ignited and used at a moment's notice. This gives the audience the feeling that they showed good judgement in coming to hear you and will ensure their return with others.

PRINCIPLES
1. Listen to your own voice often.
2. Ask for the opinion of others.
3. Use dramatics at the right time.
4. Never shout, modulate often.
5. Use emotion accurately — don't cry or be angry all the time.
6. Remember to act out your role.
7. Smile but never laugh aloud.
8. Take care with jokes and *ad-libbing*.
9. Use controlled tone.

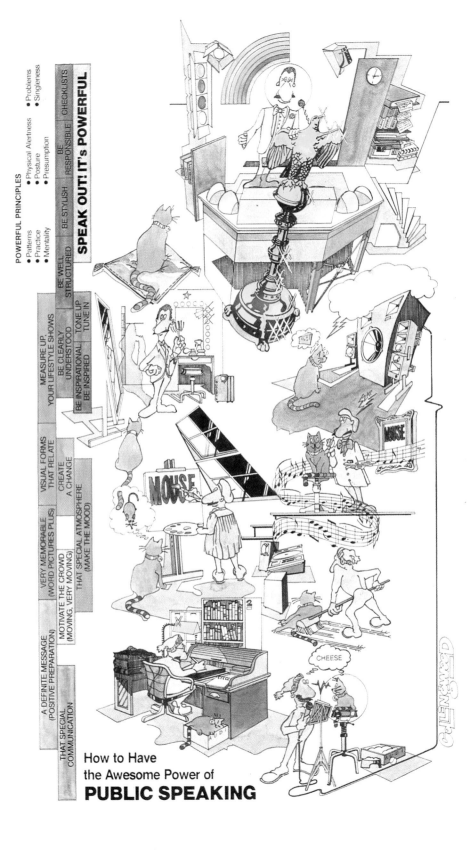

POWERFUL PRINCIPLES
- Patterns
- Practice
- Mentality
- Physical Alertness
- Posture
- Presumption
- Problems
- Singleness

SPEAK OUT! IT's POWERFUL

| BE WELL STRUCTURED | BE STYLISH | BE RESPONSIBLE | CHECKLISTS |

MEASURE UP, YOUR LIFESTYLE SHOWS		
BE CLEARLY UNDERSTOOD	TONE UP TUNE IN
BE INSPIRATIONAL BE INSPIRED	

| VISUAL FORMS THAT RELATE | |
| CREATE A CHANGE | |

VERY MEMORABLE (WORD PICTURES PLUS)	
MOTIVATE THE CROWD (MOVING, VERY MOVING)	
THAT SPECIAL ATMOSPHERE (MAKE THE MOOD)	

| A DEFINITE MESSAGE (POSITIVE PREPARATION) | |
| THAT SPECIAL COMMUNICATION | |

How to Have
the Awesome Power of
PUBLIC SPEAKING

CHAPTER FIVE

Be Inspirational

Inspiration often does not need words or even music. It can be an idea, an opinion or even a kind of eavesdropping on a special atmosphere. So a speaker must learn to catch this elusive but necessary quality and project it.

CHAPTER FIVE

Be Inspirational

Inspiration! That elusive quality that leaves you feeling warm and exhilarated after a penetrating talk or a satisfying night at the theatre!

Inspiration often does not need words or even music. It can be an idea, an opinion or even a kind of eavesdropping on a special atmosphere. So a speaker must learn to catch this elusive but necessary quality and project it, just as any great actor or actress does at the appropriate moment.

I have numerous 'attention-getters' and am continually on the lookout for others that I can use to get the attention of an audience on any occasion. Sometimes an attention-getting situation presents itself through the atmosphere of the occasion; but beware of missing the mark and handicapping the rest of your talk because of a bad start. I usually try it out on a less auspicious occasion and measure its effect before using it on a large crowd. A beginning that is an attention-getter will lay the foundation for an inspiring address and will give your audience an expectancy on which you can capitalise.

After using your attention getter, you must maintain an interesting flow of words, related to your attention getter but moving up towards your main thrust till you reach your climax. Many speakers begin with an attention getter but then lose ground by not realising that it *is* only the commencement. The rest of the speech must move upwards from that point and that is why changing to a higher gear is necessary.

It is at this point that your audience needs to feel your mood. If you are excited or sad, you need to relay that message to them in tone, posture or words. This enables them to feel what you feel and to be where you are.

As you study the great orators of today and years gone by, you will find that they not only allowed you to participate in their mood, but they also moved your deepest emotion. As you watched and listened to them, you may have laughed or cried as you were drawn along with their mood. Although Churchill, Martin Luther King Jnr., Billy Sunday or Billy Graham, to name just a few, *did not lose control*, you may have observed, on very rare occasions, a glistening in the eyes, or a smile on their lips. But they never became the object of emotion but rather the initiator. The initiator is in control and must know and direct the path ahead.

There is a profound difference between a lecture and a speech and the differences are very marked and should be clearly understood. A lecture is usually verbalising from a set of notes, principles or a formula for an audience that must respond by way of an exam, paper or a report. In essence it is *recited* by the speaker. A speech is very different and must have many more elements and display much more ability in communicating the information with persuasion and feeling; hence it is *delivered*.

One of the easiest ways to inspire your audience is to suggest a form of participation connected to your subject. This could be by way of an immediate response such as applause or standing. Or you could suggest involvement at a later date. Be very careful that it does not backfire and you find you are the initiator of something bigger than you expected and so find yourself in hot water with some government authority!

Many years ago, with some others, I spoke to a group which led to 12,000 people marching in protest. Thankfully it was ordered and well received; but it could have quite easily got out of hand with some over-enthusiastic zealots. Crowd response is much easier to start than to stop. So always make sure that the form of participation you suggest has predictability or controllable results.

When seeking to create inspiration, endeavour to deliver illustrations that are alive and plausible. Look for illustrations that can be applied to all people, describing what they are or what they would like to be. Any general or specific illustration of this kind can be used with a certain amount of safety. Wherever possible use illustrations which relate to actual events, past or present. They should lead into your final conclusion, and be related to the form of participation you desire. Paint word pictures and promote the use of imagination with suggestions hinting at the possibility of reward or danger in respect to the desired outcome.

As you build your persuasive plan and woo your audience by illustrations, facts, suggestions and presentations, a point must be reached where you can exercise some authority. This means, of course, that you have gained their confidence and earned the right to say or promote thoughts and actions that achieve your ultimate goal. The right to make such demands on an audience, however subtle or direct, must not only be timed correctly in respect to the argument you have built, but it must also be right in regard to the feel and mood of the crowd. This can sometimes be judged by the response you are getting — applause, even smaller sounds of agreement or support, body posture or eye contact. But make *very* sure that the assessment made is absolutely correct.

This assured sense of the correct time develops through years of experience. You can then even prejudge a crowd and write a speech that gives you the right to make demands on the minds of the audience at a given time, and be absolutely correct.

The conclusion of your speech must include the final blow which will tip off the scaffolding any remaining debris in the minds of your audience, so that no argument of consequence is left unanswered. But it must be done carefully because the audience's response to your final blow may wipe out any mistake or errors of omission or commission that caused a flaw in your presentation.

The finale must have awesome power and a powerful crescendo. This can take many forms. You may have seen news items on television showing a dictator or someone pushing a particular cause. You will usually find that they finish their speech with a loud, provocative claim or call to action. The reason they do it so often is that it works!

While there may be very few instances where a great, loud, provocative closing action can be used by a public speaker, it may not be wise to use it. There are certainly other methods of creating the dynamism you require. A close can be quiet, with words slowly and deliberately chosen. Or it could be something said in a whisper that trails off to a close as you quietly slip away before the crowd takes hold of the challenge and realises you have gone; then suddenly the whole stadium erupts into a standing, tumultuous ovation — when that happens whether you have closed loudly or quietly and thoughtfully, you have won the day and your job is well done!

PRINCIPLES
1. Start with an attention getter.
2. Keep the flow modulated but upward in direction.
3. Allow your audience to feel your mood.
4. Move the deepest emotion.
5. Suggest a form of participation.
6. Deliver living and imaginable illustrations.
7. Finish with a great crescendo, loud, quiet, angry or thoughtful.

Motivate Your Audience

You program your audience. You are, as it were, a potter with clay, fashioning a unique type of mind set by what you say.

CHAPTER SIX

Motivate
Your Audience

In every speech a certain moment of convincing needs to be achieved in the early stages. It may well be that your audience is already on your side, but I would suggest that at an early stage in your presentation you plant the seed thought that you would like to be the final thrust of your speech. In other words, 'sow the seed and then sell the need.' If you can move the audience into your frame of reference early, then you have begun well.

You *program* your audience. You are, as it were, a potter with clay, fashioning a unique type of mind set by what you say. As I said earlier, you have a certain power just because you are the speaker. You can ask your audience to stand up, turn around, put their left hand up, shake hands with the person next to them or any number of things. This gives you the opening to take it further, until you either convince your audience by your presentation or your tone or you turn them off through the lack of it.

To get your audience on side, always try to start with a point you know they will agree with. Then move skilfully towards the main thrust of your message. But several times during the talk bring your message back to an agreed point to keep your audience with you and so get their willing participation.

When making a point that requires a *change* in the mind set of your audience, always make the problem seem easy to correct. This will help to remove any negative feeling towards your suggestion. An easy way to get your audience interested is to reinterpret an existing principle from a different viewpoint, using a different tone of voice than is normally used and with a different emphasis on certain words. I am not suggesting that you misinterpret the principle, but rather dissect it and take a fresh approach, showing insight into an old principle.

If I had a particularly demanding speaking appointment, I would spend at least a full day at the public library writing down the key elements of my message, and then with determined concentration seek to provide the audience with something fresh to take home or back to their office to share with others. Every principle has within its structure thoughts and elements of comprehension that need to be reaffirmed. What better way can you do it than by providing a new and challenging aspect that has not been expressed before!

Do not be daunted by the task ahead of you. Just believe that a new concept or thought is possible and write it down quickly before it can escape from your mind.

Many years ago I thought up a new concept in behavioural science and became so excited I pushed my thought patterns for the *complete* concept, only to lose the initial key thoughts because I did not write them down quickly. It was another seven years before I recaptured those initial thoughts. Then I wrote them down instantly!

To bring about a change or confirm a principle use a true example, either from the past or from current events, to illustrate. You can even speculate in story form about what could happen. The key to public speaking is to make your concept real and let it live. Permit your audience to eavesdrop, as it were, on a life drama which is taking place before their very eyes. Sometimes it is prudent to give two or three living illustrations with consequences, good or bad, to demonstrate the value and the integrity of your concept.

When you have persuaded your audience to agree with you, by using the principles of these chapters, you need to reconvince them that they are right in feeling the way that they do. Phrases like 'you are right to have doubts about...' or 'isn't it

good to have the facts and realise that. . .'. Sometimes it becomes very pertinent to use a local
illustration to bring home a living truth; but be
extremely sure of your facts because a local situation has many facets and can alienate some
because they sometimes know the real story
behind the public relations report.

There are many different ways to move an
audience in the direction you want them to go. I
will list just a few which can be expanded upon
according to your own creativity.

1. *The No Option Choice*
At the appropriate time in your speech, as you
build up your argument, the words *'we have no
other choice. . .'* will confirm the direction you are
taking. But these words must include 'we', and not
'you', because you have to build togetherness and
confirm the bond you have with your audience. If
you use this approach, always add something
extra to your argument to confirm your claim.

2. *Motivation by Self Interest*
I would like to point out that self interest is quite
different to selfishness. Self interest has more to do
with survival and protection whereas selfishness
involves withholding from others. Self interest is
always compelling because it directs itself to the
heart of all human need.

The key words at the appropriate time here are,

'you need to. . .' this again is directed towards the audience but in a way that makes you become as it were, their protective benefactor.

3. *Motivation by Knowledge*
   This form of motivation of an audience can be very convincing if you present it in such a way that it seems you are letting them eavesdrop on surprising, exclusive information. You confirm something which is known by the crowd only because they are so clever. The active words are, 'you are aware that' — and then present the information.

4. *Motivation by Guilt*
   This must be used with care, but it is a powerful motivational tool that always gets a response from your audience. 'How would you feel if. . .' the emphasis here is put on *'you'*. This is the active word which gets the guilt involvement moving.

5. *Motivation by Fear*
   This form of motivation is the most easily used because it is negative. To think and act negatively requires a great deal less energy and thought than to initiate courage, and so therefore it can be used to great effect. It can be used in the singular, collective form and be directed towards family, employment and many other areas of life. It ultimately means survival in its sharpest and some-

times most desperate form.

As is the case with all these motivational thrusts it has a trigger. The words are 'You'll be hurt. . . if you do. . .'. These words must be expressed with concern or in a protective, outraged tone.

6. *Motivation by Conscience*
    To use this to full effect, almost everything has to be perfect, and action must be initiated almost immediately. It is so difficult to motivate by conscience because conscience adjusts so quickly and a commitment to do or not to do something in response is easily rationalised. To use this motivation to its best effect it may pay to include a fear or self interest suggestion to give it more power and permanence. The emphasis here is, 'You cannot allow. . . to happen. . .'

All of these motivational thrusts must be aimed at the individual although spoken to the total audience. What usually happens is that each person senses that you are talking to someone else in the crowd, but it could somehow indirectly apply to them. Be very careful not to aim your words, accusations or demands so directly that each person feels you are speaking only to him, because, although it is acceptable and even desirable to do so in most public speaking, an accusing or demanding pronouncement may bring a totally defensive result, which means you have not only missed the mark but you have permanently lost your audience.

Use the slightly evasive side door method which makes defense from your audience indefensible. Be alert, be sensitive, be disciplined, be sure and be sensational!

PRINCIPLES
1. Get your audience on side first.
2. Motivate by demand.
3. Motivate by self interest.
4. Motivate by knowledge.
5. Motivate by guilt.
6. Motivate by fear.
7. Motivate by conscience.

Underline the Message

It is much easier to speak to an audience that is on your side. You can then underline your message either in words or with some visual aids.

CHAPTER SEVEN

Underline the Message

It is much easier to speak to an audience that is on your side. You can then underline your message either in words or with some visual aids.

But win them over first. Use simplicity, with romance, to captivate your audience. Be creative but not raucous in your style.

For instance, it would be foolish to use a loud display of action at a senior citizens' gathering; but it *would* be very appropriate to extol some great achievement of the past and tell of its greatness and help to mankind, using facts and figures to illustrate, and then compliment the pioneers of the past for their ingenuity and courage against the odds.

Once I was asked to speak to a group of women. I commenced by naming about 20 women in succession who throughout the ages had contributed to the world by their creative ability and sacrifice.

Paul J. Meyer once addressed a large audience.

He placed two large fans on the stage, turned them on, and then threw 2000 dollar bills in the air. The audience went wild picking them up under chairs and catching them in the air. Paul went on to explain that people everywhere were busy picking up dollar bills and overlooking their capacity to earn a great deal more by setting goals. Paul then gave a brilliant talk on goal setting and sold his excellent programs, which he produces under the name 'Success Motivation Institute'. Use drama for the appropriate occasion and watch your audience respond with delight and acclamation.

Sometimes, on special occasions, it is appropriate to irritate the conscience. Many of us overlook the benefits we have in the country we live in and take a great deal for granted. If you are speaking to seek donations or assistance for a worthy cause, you need to paint word pictures and relate to the lack of thought which puts your audience in the picture. Then you can include a conscience jolt that produces the required response.

Creating a special mood requires certain principles that must be adhered to. The first principle is the quality of the introduction. If this goes badly, don't be wiped out but get on with your presentation without missing a beat or shaking your head or showing any concern whatever, because any concern, irritation or panic is immediately transferred to your audience and everybody feels uncomfortable.

Some years ago, when everything at the beginning went wrong, I good-naturedly suggested to the organizers and the audience that we start it again. I went off stage and the organisers did the introductions again and everything went fine.

You are in such a privileged position as a public speaker that you can set, change or destroy a mood. Recently in Brisbane, Australia, I was asked to address a particularly rowdy group of teenage delinquents who had demonstrated with gusto their ability to annihilate the most experienced speaker with loud swearing, fights and thrown objects. I was firmly warned and even given the opportunity to back out of the assignment several times, but I agreed to go. The group was indeed boisterous, and as I was being fitted with my radio microphone I was again offered escape. But I am happy to report that all went very well and I had one of the quietest and one of the most responsive groups ever because I sought to control them rather than have them control me.

This is what happened.

After the organisers introduced me (with some difficulty because of the noise), I walked quietly onto the centre stage and, without looking to the front, I took out a ten dollar bill, unfolded it with obvious and deliberate calm, held it up slightly for all to see, and then placed it on a table where it could be observed by all present. Then I took out two more with the same deliberation and calm, at no time looking at the audience. I was preoccupied with the deliberations of the moment. I then spoke firmly and directly to the young people and told them that the three ten dollar bills were for the three quietest people in the hall — only to have a young smart alec call out some obscenity. I told him he was disqualified and then quickly said, 'But I will give you another chance.' This meant he could compete rather than become disruptive and cause a ruckus throughout the talk. The response was unbelievable and even after the talk, when I had given out the three ten dollar bills, we had a 45 minute question time held with great dignity, sincerity and intelligence.

If you ever are interrupted in a speech, leave it to the organisers to correct the situation. If it is someone agitating against you personally and no-one comes to your rescue, you can either sit down or use it to your advantage by

1. Suggesting to the intruder that he adhere to the rules of etiquette and wait until he is invited to speak.
2. Debating him on the spot.
3. Seeking help from the audience to clap him or her down with slow claps.
4. Going on with your talk without even recognising the intruder.

It is foolish to try and move a crowd without some elementary research about your subject to substantiate your claim. A simple way is to illustrate long and short term consequences, good or bad according to the occasion. But remember that the negative statement, because of its element of fear, is always more powerful than the positive, which requires more proof and drama to ignite the flame of action.

Always produce profound proof and predictions, and quote from actual documents to make your point. I saw a dramatic illustration of this on television recently when a politician was confronted by his opponent with a ten foot long scroll of broken promises which, of course, annihilated any argument to the contrary.

As you move through your talk try and create conclusions which are logical and reasonable. Seek some point of agreement with your audience by affirming their intelligence with words such as 'the only reasonable conclusion that can be drawn from these facts is... and I am sure you agree with this.'

At times I have even reduced the problem to a mathematical problem using a whiteboard or overhead transparency to create a formula that can be easily followed. Always make your formula easy to grasp. Try it out on a number of people beforehand to get reaction.

One of the most powerful methods I have used to make my point is to create a poem, rhyme or ditty, either humorous or serious. I have been blessed with a special gift for this and can usually do something quite satisfactory in one or two minutes; but I am sure almost anyone could do it with perseverance. If you really want to make an impact with your poem, rhyme or ditty, have it handed out as people leave.

PRINCIPLES
1. Win your audience with simplicity and romance.
2. Use drama if appropriate.
3. Irritate the conscience if appropriate.
4. Handle interruptions with confidence.
5. Create logical conclusions.
6. Reduce the problem to an easy formula.
7. Cap off your speech with a poem, rhyme or ditty.

Say it with Style

In any communication you must get the other person's attention at the beginning. For a public speaker it is no different

CHAPTER EIGHT

Say it with Style!

Whenever you speak always get the preliminaries right. Honour those to whom honour is due. (Do not leave this to guess work. Ask your sponsor if there are any dignitaries present and how they should be addressed.) Give compliments and thanks to those special people who do all the work.

Your own introduction has some importance, although I used to adopt the attitude that if I do not produce the goods the introduction will not help. But on many of the occasions when I was fortunate enough to be at my best, I overheard people say, 'Who is this guy?' So some essentials of introduction are important. Some speakers have a pro-forma introduction which can be read out and I'm sure that is helpful.

I believe that the best introduction comes from someone who personally knows the speaker or who is familiar with his or her writings or achievements, because then a certain amount of sincerity flows out which gives an introduction a kind of credibility. This in turn creates an air of anticipation in the audience.

All introductions, however complimentary, are rendered useless if the speaker does not follow through with the goods and relate to the topic intimately. If you really do not communicate, you have virtually insulted the promoters.

In any communication you must get the other person's attention at the beginning. For a public speaker it is no different. Some break the preoccupational barrier by telling a joke or some startling unknown fact.

I once opened my talk to a large insurance audience by walking onto the stage and for 30 seconds saying nothing. Then I proclaimed,

'I want to tell you this morning that you are all overpaid!'

I paused to let them catch their breath and then went on in an appealing dramatic tone,

'All commission salespeople are overpaid because commissions are set for mediocrity.'

Pause again. And then in a higher tone,

'Any fool can beat mediocrity!'

The attention getting effect was explosive and created an air of expectancy which carried through the whole session. Always follow through that kind of commencement with a strong comment on an issue that your audience agrees with.

This will keep them on your side, ready for some other pronouncement that may not be as palatable.

Mix facts with drama to get your message across and watch your audience respond with vigour. Some time ago I had to speak on motivation to senior executives who were starting to wind down and looking to do less, rather than more. I searched the libraries to find those who had achieved remarkable feats of endurance and success in many varied fields after they were 80 years old and even up to 100 years of age.

When I spoke, I emphasised the disabilities they had to contend with and, in sequence, almost barked out their names, ages and achievements in a long list. At the end I asked the question, 'What's your problem?' Pause. 'Are you trying to be an excusiologist?' The response was unbelievable and has worked just as well anywhere in the world.

The interesting thing I have found in my frequent travels around the world is that wisdom and humour are transnational and, used in the right context, cross all cultural barriers.

There are certain times in a speech when you can create applause exactly where and when you want it. It has to do with content and timing. For example you build up to a crescendo, then drop in a challenge or a point of agreement in some short dramatic sentence, then just wait and invariably your audience will respond with acclaim.

Experience will show you how and when to do it and will also help you perfect it. During one particular speech of 45 minutes I was fortunate enough to trigger that kind of response 25 times.

A very simple but effective way to create a good speech is used by some preachers and lecturers but not to its ultimate value. Use a point or principle system. Pick out three to five points that you would like to convey to your audience and name them with your emphasis on point 1, point 2 and so on until you get through each of them. Reaffirm them at the conclusion so that your audience is left in no doubt as to what you want to convey to them in respect to the principles involved.

Occasionally in a talk an audience is taken by surprise by the way the speaker relates to a subject. It is at these times that you should feel you are in a position to relate to the unrelatable. In other words, move from one position to an entirely unrelated position and then back again, creating a relationship that has never been expressed or recognised before. Be realistic and accurate but think, think, think in unrelated terms to get your point across.

Always pay attention to style. Just as a sportsman has a particular style in the way he plays the game, so you must develop your own individual style. Whereas you may learn from others and improve on their gestures and performance, endeavour to create your own style related to the general message you deliver and relevant to your own personality.

Just as John Wayne had a particular walk and voice style, so we all have our own style of gestures and delivery; but attention needs to be paid to development and growth in our continual presentation.

PRINCIPLES
1. Get the preliminaries right — acknowledge dignitaries — check those who are involved.
2. The beginning must get attention — create an air of expectancy.
3. Find some points of agreement.
4. Give facts and dramatise them.
5. Emphasis followed by silence brings a response.
6. Follow through on a point or principle system.
7. Relate to the unrelatable for memorable effect.
8. Develop a style that is unforgettable.

CHAPTER NINE

Have a Deep Sense of Responsibility

To speak to any group, whether large or small, carries with it a deep responsibility.
A professional speaker's personal principles are never up for sale.

CHAPTER NINE

Have a Deep Sense of Responsibility

To speak to any group, whether large or small, carries with it a deep sense of responsibility. Special care must always be taken in respect to the material you present because cassette tapes, videos, notes and word of mouth can continue for many years after the event and what has been said can often hang around as long as a 30 year mortgage to identify and quantify the validity of what has been said.

Careful research and clarification must be skilfully and meticulously produced to present truth and knowledge that will stand and be continually vindicated by the test of time. Casual theories and idle chatter have no place on the professional speaker's platform and responsibility must be felt, with a certain degree of sincerity, before any words are to be uttered from the speaker's lips.

One of the most distinguishing factors between an amateur and a professional speaker is the style,

clarity and originality of the material presented.
To borrow or use segments of other people's work
to substantiate a fact or emphasise a point is
allowable, and sometimes very appropriate and
useful, but to steal another speaker's context or
material indicates a lack of character and knowledge.

As I move around the world I am continually
confronted by speakers and would be speakers
who have little or no material of their own but
continually and recklessly use and abuse other
people's knowledge without reference and without permission. I suppose the worst area of
espionage is in the area of leadership, which tends
to be part of every speaker's package, yet an
obvious question that has never really been
asked, 'What, if anything, has the speaker done
that he or she is drawing illustrations or principles
from?'

I once witnessed a particularly blatant example of
this. A speaker had given a somewhat hesitant and
jumpy talk on leadership, and when he stopped for a
cup of coffee, there on the seat next to him were two
books on leadership from which he obtained the
major points for his talk, without any reference at all
to the author or the books!

Stealing from others shows itself with abundant
clarity at a gruelling question time when an active
audience can pale the most articulate speaker but
rarely cause a ripple in the composure of the per-

formance of the experienced professional.

A sense of responsibility must also be exercised in respect to the allotted time on the platform. I always ask how much time I have and then ask what time I have to finish by; rarely do these times coincide! So clarify what happens if anything goes overtime, which it usually does. Do not under any circumstance accept a response of laughter or a 'put off' when asking what happens if the proceedings go overtime, but rather insist quietly but firmly on a formula to solve the problem and repeat it back to the person in control.

If there is more than one speaker or other items make doubly sure that you do not take any time from someone else, as they deserve and have been given an allotted time and should expect to fulfil it. To steal someone else's time on the platform is considered the worst of manners and ensures a bad reputation and long term alienation from other speakers and performers.

Sometime ago I was contacted by telephone from Sydney asking if I had a vacancy to speak at a rather large gala affair in about six weeks time. I discussed fees, travel and accommodation arrangements and seemed to reach a point of general agreement till I asked the question, 'What do you want me to promote?' The answer came back 'Poker machines.'

My response was, 'You've lost yourself a speaker!'

The gentleman in question was well mannered but persistent, but to no avail. I have some very strong views about gambling, alcohol, drugs and illicit sex and will not under any circumstances promote or be seen to endorse any of them.

The rule is that a professional speaker's personal principles are never up for sale. The obvious, but rarely recognised, feature of a public speaker is that once he starts to speak he is in total, absolute control and everyone, including the organizers, is at his mercy.

I was compering a large meeting once that, although large and significant and of much public importance, could not get any attention or coverage from the media. On the opening night of the meetings in question, I told the huge audience that I had contacted the media and they said that they were not interested. I asked the audience to phone the newspapers the next morning and tell them how much we appreciated them and how important they were in our community.

The following morning I had a visit from the newspapers and they said that their phones had been jammed with callers, all of goodwill, which had prevented them from doing their normal business. Needless to say that night at the meeting we had all the media present and it was well reported the next day. A direct example of platform power.

If you have set a goal to be a public speaker, then you must not be disappointed in the early stages at the occasional flop. Even experienced speakers sometimes bomb out and miss the target in respect to the mood, geographics or theme of what was anticipated by the crowd. When you flop, and everytime you miss the mark or are dissatisfied with your performance, you must emotionally examine yourself. There are no bad audiences, only bad, misinformed or unprepared speakers. Your responsibility to your craft and to humanity as a whole should always demand your best, and in doing so you will create for yourself the awesome power of public speaking.

PRINCIPLES
1. Research your material.
2. Do not steal from others.
3. Maintain integrity regarding time on the platform.
4. Don't sell yourself for a pittance (or anything else).
5. You are and must always be in control.
6. A flop must not stop you.

CHAPTER TEN

Evaluate, Evaluate

What would you think of a carpenter without a ruler, or a mathematician without a number, or a bank without a balance sheet? Ridiculous, isn't it! How much more ridiculous is it to take your public speaking seriously yet fail to have a measuring stick.

CHAPTER TEN

Evaluate, Evaluate

I want to highlight the absolute necessity of deciding on a way of measuring as accurately as possible your success or failure in working toward your goal of possessing the awesome power of public speaking.

What would you think of a carpenter without a ruler, or a mathematician without a number, or a bank without a balance sheet? Ridiculous, isn't it! How much more ridiculous is it to take your public speaking seriously yet fail to have a measuring stick. Develop a simple check list and grade yourself against it. Here's something to start with:

1. Number and length of acclamations.
2. Recommendations or return invitations.
3. Letters of appreciation received.
4. Fees paid.
5. Books or tapes sold.
6. Increase in the number of return visits.

And so the list could go on.

But already during your speech you can begin to assess the response you are getting. Look for facial and other expressions that indicate to you the level of acceptance you are getting. If people start to yawn, fidget, talk to each other, move around or move out, you know you are in deep trouble and you had better say something interesting, dramatic or funny quickly to get the attention back and break the preoccupational barriers.

The response you need is head nodding, clapping, cheers, note taking, leaning forward, and so on. But the best response is to have your audience stare at you, in a forward posture, silent and unmoving. To the beginner it is unnerving and very unsettling because you feel as though you are speaking to zombies, but in fact you are experiencing in its final and most powerful form the absolutely awesome power of public speaking.

Very often after a session like this some speakers are alarmed because, although they may get a thunderous standing ovation, they find that afterwards in the foyer, talking to members of the audience, they get very little response. People can be overawed or stunned by what you have to say or the way in which you present it. For the average speaker, who only speaks from time to time, it may be difficult to assess the difference between an audience ignoring you in the foyer because you did not perform to their expectations, and a similar response from them when they have been stirred or wiped out emotionally by the speaker's awesome power of public speaking.

The most effective way of evaluating whether your message was clearly understood is to spend some time with the audience afterwards. One of the principles that I endeavour to pursue in my many talks around the world is to walk around and meet as many people as I can afterwards and question them politely in respect to their comments. If someone tells me that they found the talk helpful or inspirational then I would ask them to be more specific — *what* was helpful or what principle did they find so applicable. I make mental notes of what is said, but I pursue my questioning with polite vigour until I have a very good idea of the mood of the audience and that which helped create such a mood. Be careful of critics who will try to wipe you out with a put down. Experience will show you what is said in truth and what is correct compared to what is said merely to create despair.

If someone suggests to you that your speech was 'wonderful' or 'dynamic', don't be too bashful to ask them what particularly appealed to them and whether they would appreciate more time in the speech for that item next time.

Of course the other indication of your degree of success is the number and types of letters you receive. It takes a great deal more resolve to sit down and write to a speaker than make a casual or courteous comment at the venue.

I often meet people who tell me of their great speaking prowess; but when I ask them how much people are prepared to pay to hear them (a loaded question), the response is often very empty indeed. If an audience is prepared to pay an entrance fee to hear you speak, particularly if they have heard you before, you have a strong indication that you are successfully entertaining or meeting a need.

Beware of the concluding remarks of the Master of Ceremonies whose task it is to praise and thank the speaker. While what is said in appreciation may well be true, it is nevertheless simply expected manners to be complimentary. The most reliable source of encouragement and compliment is a quick invitation in writing with dates and fees set for a return performance. Nothing can be said that negates the power and positive acclamation of that.

When you are invited back on these conditions again and again, then no other credentials are needed. You have indeed mastered the 'Awesome Power of Public Speaking'.

PRINCIPLES
1. Develop methods of evaluation.
2. Assess response and adapt accordingly.
3. The best response is a return invitation.

CHAPTER ELEVEN

Check Your Lifestyle

The great speakers of this world are achievers in their fields and because of that not only have the opportunity to speak but the right to be heard

CHAPTER ELEVEN

Check Your Lifestyle

I was approached by a very keen, good looking young man with stars in his eyes who posed the question 'How do I get onto the public speaking circuit?' I asked him what message he had to offer. He said he could speak on whatever was wanted. After further questioning, I found he was under the mistaken impression that public speaking was just a matter of being able to tell an audience something which is either stolen from others or simply imaginative, rather than coming from the pain and anguish of experience.

The young man in question was something of a failure in many areas. He made the common mistake of thinking that you can be a success just by talking to others about it. I told him that I did not know of any particular speaker's circuit and suggested that he first create a platform of success from which he would be eagerly heard.

I am disappointed when I hear of public speakers who *say* but do not *do*, because it is dishonest and sooner or later will prove them shallow. The great speakers of this world are achievers in their fields and because of that not only have the opportunity to speak but the right to be heard.

I was once in northern Queensland, in the crocodile area of Australia, taking a weekend of seminars. On the way back to the airport, my host said to me, 'Thank you for being real. I had heard so much about your achievements, but nothing about your personality and genuineness.' It was the nicest compliment I have ever received.

Don't be a phoney. Be real and live the life you proclaim. Set out to achieve, continually pitching yourself against the commercial and human elements of this world in an effort to succeed, despite the temporary setbacks that keep you in touch with the realities of life.

Wherever you go remember that you are *always* in the spotlight. People who have heard you speak feel they have some kind of ownership towards you, so always take care that you are well dressed and well groomed.

When speaking, allow your audience to discover something of your personality by using personal illustrations. An example which comes to mind is a television advertisement we were preparing for our real estate company. I was planning to do a personal front-on dialogue to my viewing audience. My eldest son, who works with me, said,

'Dad, why don't you let the people see you as we do, jogging through the roses in the park in the morning, and then talk.' I thought Peter junior was crazy, but when we tested it the response was fantastic. To this day people come up to me in the streets and in shops and ask me if I still run. It seems as if there was something about my being a jogger in the park that my audience could identify with.

It is also important to recognise the help you have received from others. One of the hardest principles to get across to speakers is the need to give credit to others where it is due and thereby share your success. I will never forget the encouragement I have received from others. In a very real way they have played a major role in my speaking activity — those who tirelessly pulled crowds together, arranged lighting and sound, sold my books and gave hospitality are but a few of the great army of participants in my life. I always seek to give credit to others from the platform to underline my appreciation of the support and assistance given. Sometimes I even ask those people to stand up or come up onto the platform for all to see. Those small but important courtesies are part and parcel of your role as a speaker and should not be neglected at any time.

It is often important when speaking before a group to give credibility to what you say. On one occasion I was speaking before a large insurance group on motivation. I emphasised the need for a daily affirmation card which should be read daily to affirm your goals and those things that you hold as your life's principle and philosophy. I reached into my wallet and pulled out my own affirmation card and held it up for all to see. The response was overwhelming. Afterwards a large number of executives and sales people were pushing through to ask to see my card, and although I would not let them read it because of its very personal nature, I still displayed it again for all to see. As public speakers we very often have to demonstrate our involvement in what we are speaking about.

PRINCIPLES
1. Be real; live the life you are proclaiming.
2. You must always look right (in tone and tune with your surroundings).
3. Give personal illustrations, share your life with the audience.
4. Give credit to others.
5. Demonstrate involvement related to speech.

CHAPTER TWELVE

How the Awesome Power is Unleashed

There are other elements that remain a mystery to us all and cannot be suitably explained. They remain locked up in the vault of the supernatural to which only God has the key. It is His good pleasure to unlock and release such power to a chosen few.

CHAPTER TWELVE

How the Awesome Power is Unleashed

Like any other occupation in life public speaking has specific proven elements that make it work. At times some of these elements can be avoided, ignored or discarded with very little effect upon the final product. But to be a *professional* in public speaking, as with all who determine to be masters of their craft, all the known elements must not only be used but they must be sharpened to the finest edge to produce a quality that can only be applied to those who bear the title of awesome.

However, there are other elements that remain a mystery to us all and cannot be suitably explained. They remain locked up in the vault of the supernatural to which only God has the key. It is His good pleasure to unlock and release such power to a chosen few. The following, final principles are proven and tried in the heat of battle on the world stage of judgements and acclamations.

More could and will be written in the future. But I can say with candor and transparency that I have given all. If there are still lessons to be learned then I shall have to learn them. And if there are mysteries to be unlocked, then I'll leave that to almighty God and His great wisdom and love. My prayer is that should these principles of power fall into the hands of the tyrant, dictator, or the Elmer Gantries of this world, then may God render them useless and void of power.

The Pattern of Power

As in any game or power play a pattern must be produced to maximise the effectiveness of that which needs to be done. So it is in public speaking. Let me summarise some of these areas again.

The first element to be addressed in public speaking is a clear, simple mission statement about what you expect to achieve through your message. This statement should not exceed 50 words and must be honed with clarity and force to the accurate substance of what you want to say and what effect you want it to have.

The second element is the division of your presentation into numbered principles or points that will clearly identify the progress and the fundamentals of your theme.

The third element is the research which adds weight to what you have to say with authoritative statements or quotes by others who would be acceptable to your audience.

The fourth element would be the written layout of all your material into an easy flow of communicating words that will draw the conclusion you desire.

The final element is evaluation and production of a voice sound and emphasis suitable for each phrase and emphasis that gives some added meaning to the words you say.

The Principles of Power

In the early stages of public speaking one is apt to go anywhere one is asked. Indeed, it becomes an opportunity to grapple with oneself and the audience, to learn and experiment.

I would suggest even at an early stage of your entry into the arena of public speaking that you develop a set of principles that are unmovable in respect to what you stand for as a person and what you believe is needed to be done in this world and beyond to further enhance the lives of those you come in contact with.

Whilst it is true that I am almost prepared to speak to any group of people, there are certain things I will not promote and there are certain principles I will never violate. My commitment as a Christian allows me great freedom and opportunity but also has within that framework certain restrictions and obligations that I accept gladly. To have the awesome power of public speaking carries with it prestige, insights, and wealth but it also carries the additional obligations of responsibility for how it is used. Remember that power is a double edged sword that can build or destroy not only others, but also yourself.

The Practice of Power

No great sculptor, musician, surgeon or actor can perform consistently well without practice. So it is with those who desire or have the awesome power of public speaking. I know of no other key to be good at anything than practice, practice, practice with relentless continuity and creative variety.

Thousands of times I have practised my talks. In the early days I would go into the country and cause the birds to stop singing with my clumsy rhetoric. At home I would often go into the bathroom and turn all the taps on full while practising for that special occasion. Often I would try and stay home alone and deliver my speech into a tape recorder and play it back, looking for those awkward sentences that needed remolding and tones and sounds that had to be rectified to create the desired flow. I even went to the extent of adding applause from other soundtracks to try and savour something of what I was expecting to experience to enable me to accept a response without getting off the track. At these times I would also listen to recordings of Dr. Martin Luther King,

Dr. Billy Graham, Billy Sunday, Sir Winston Churchill and many others to capture and try to savour
something of their oratorical genius.

The Mentality for Power

To have the correct mentality for the power to
be released from the podium is a necessary part of
professional public speaking. Very often huge
crowds induce the feeling. At other times you
have to create it for yourself. Just as a supreme
athlete psyches himself up for that record break-
ing jump, so you must prepare yourself for the all
important speech. Often before going on stage I
affirm myself with self talk to wash away the idle
chatter that has proceeded the moment and to
clear my mind and to focus on the immediate task
at hand. I never go into a speaking appointment
without prayer, realising that any unction comes
from God. I am always acutely aware that just as
Samson of old lost his power through disobe-
dience, whatever I possess can be removed both
quickly and permanently.

The problem of nervousness rarely bothers me
now, as I am so caught up in the body of the
performance required that to be nervous is not
one of the obstacles that has to be overcome; but
in the early days it plagued me constantly for over
ten years to the point of such extreme embarrassment that I had to drink a mixture of flour, milk
and sugar to ensure that my bowels were con-

trolled and gummed up before I got up to speak.

The Physical Alertness for Power

I was in Malaysia at the Genting Highland Resort at the invitation of the Great Eastern Life Assurance Company. As they were introducing me, they played punchy, dramatic music, enveloping the huge auditorium. Robina, my wife, was sitting next to me and told me to stop hurting myself. What she had observed for the first time (although I had been doing it for over 20 years) was that I was pinching my arms, legs and body hard to make me alert and vital when I hit the platform.

I am not suggesting this method for everybody but I find that it temporarily eliminates tiredness and general fatigue and creates an alertness that readies the speaker for impact.

The other alertness technique I use is fast, deep breathing. If nobody is looking, I will punch the air to get myself physically prepared, as it were, for the performance of my life. These and other body movements can and do emphasise action and create a personal atmosphere that induces alertness. I rarely run onto the stage as some speakers do, because of the lack of dignity and the possibility of falling or losing my notes or tripping over electrical cables.

The Postures of Power

General De Gaulle, Churchill, Chiang Kai-shek

— all heroes of the past but everpresent in the minds of those who admire greatness — all have what many would call the posture of power. Their walk, look, gestures and style all created a posture image that exuded power.

Whilst I do not and could never agree with the axiom 'fake it until you make it', there is, I believe, a certain dignity in the way one is presented and, even in a so called enlightened society, is admired and sometimes feared. Hanging onto a podium throughout a speech removes the posture of power as does the continual moving backwards and forwards across the stage which tends, I believe, to take away the emphasis on speech and contact.

However, there is a happy medium and power-ful posture or a set of postures that create the illusion and at times the reality of power. Sincerity can rarely be faked and a waving of the arms and body movements that are not in tune with what has been said will only take away from your mes-sage and may even make the whole thing appear ridiculous and even laughable. To make a dra-matic statement of force requires one to step back slightly from the podium, have both arms hang downwards with a slight curve and a clenched fist with a direct and determined look forward.

Body movements are difficult to program for a book because what would look good or accept-able to one might look quite the opposite for another. Study those whom you consider the best in their fields and observe the body movements which you believe give special impact and emphasis. Try to select those that relate to your style and adopt them as your very own.

Never overlook the impact of a nod of the head, a look, a body movement or stillness to create the kind of response that you have preplanned to produce.

The Presumption with Power

There are times during a speech that you have earned the right to presume. The audience have demonstrated that they are with you by their rapt attention, laughter or applause and you have measured accurately their mood and character. This allows you to make a dramatic move full of confidence and prediction.

Timing is of paramount importance in driving home with precision and accuracy the thrust of your theme to an immovable conclusion that cannot fail. It is at these times that the real pro has, as it were, a special sensitising of the moment. When the time arises to make your claim, do it with gusto and dignity. If you miss the crescendo of the crowd's acceptance, then it must be created again; but remember the second time around is more difficult and sometimes one has to accept second best rather than miss out altogether.

To time an occasion for applause or affirmation

from the audience sometimes requires just a simple, strong, agreeable statement followed by silence to achieve your aim. The more times you speak, the more times you practise and the better you prepare, the more accurately you will know how to use timing and silence to your advantage. Remember, dignity of style and a deliberate choice of words with a sense of timing which expects results will often win the day.

The Problems of Power

I was travelling once with a famous speaker. He kept telling me how much he had to avoid people at airports because he would be recognised and people would bother him. As we walked through the airport terminal together nobody noticed him and indeed even the receptionist of the V.I.P. room did not recognise who he was. My companion was quite put out and kept looking around and smiling at anyone whose eye he could catch. Finally he walked out of the V.I.P. room with the weak excuse that he needed a particular magazine. He continued to walk up and down the air terminal passenger lounge until he was noticed.

How sad, I thought, that a person needs to be stroked and praised and noticed continually to feel secure. Other people of fame I have known demand and very often get extra special service and attention far beyond their comfort needs, at the same time embarrassing those around them and abusing the privileges extended to them because of their popularity, power or prominence.

It is not only bad manners but also arrogant to use a position of power, prominence or popularity to control, manipulate or make demands upon others. If you are successful in your quest for the awesome power of public speaking, that, I believe, does not turn the liberty you have developed and been given into a license for frivolity or arrogance. Whilst at times you do your best and, because of certain pressures, you may need some special attention, such privileges should be received and welcomed with a gratitude attitude, showing you are aware that your public, in a sense, made you and keep you where you are and can just as easily bring you down to earth.

Beware of power and realise its ability to seduce. Recognise and resist its capacity to make you something you are not.

The Singleness of Power

There are those very rare occasions brought about by extraordinary means where you break all the rules and still come out winning. It happens in sport, political elections, and business, and public speaking is no exception. The thing to remember is that these *are* exceptions and to be exceptions they must by virtue of that title be quite elusive. I have witnessed only once or twice in my lifetime that rare occasion when the speaker was ill prepared to respond to a spontaneous occasion but somehow did the unique and the unpredictable that made his speech a communication masterpiece.

Never ever rely or expect that to happen and hope somehow it will win the day. For those who read this book to obtain some help for the occasional speaking assignment then let me say that all the principles in this book apply to you and it is simply a matter of evaluating just how serious you are about that speaking appointment. That will determine how dedicated you are to achieving excellence. Very often an excellent delivery, concept or script alone can carry one through but to use any one by itself without emphasis on the other two would be fraught with danger.

The speech you give on whatever subject to whatever audience is a simple but clear declaration that you have ideals, thoughts and concepts that you are prepared to put up for scrutiny and on that basis you are challenging your audience to judge you. And judge they will!

So my final words to all who read this book and aspire to greatness — speak on with awesome power!

APPENDIX A

Those Forgotten Extras

1. Check for clean drinking water.
2. Make sure you toilet.
3. Eat raw, fresh pineapple if your throat is thick or you have a cold. You will find it will clear it up quickly and certainly sufficiently to enable you to make your speech.
4. Remove nametags or badges that will reflect from the stage.
5. Plan your exit to allow you to get backstage or wherever you have to go at the conclusion.
6. Be very careful of steps and ramps, particularly after coming off the stage when your eyes have been used to the spotlight.
7. Make sure you can read your notes and that they are at the right height and slant so that your audience does not have to look at the crown of your head.

8. Check the podium for stability.
9. Make sure your notes do not slip or blow away.
10. Keep away from fans, heaters and air conditioners.
11. Check all sound systems throughout the room.
12. Check that the event is still on well before you arrive.
13. Remember that big audiences are much easier to handle than small audiences.
14. Double check the time and length of the speech.
15. Ask whoever is in charge for a program to enable you to understand when and where you come on.
16. Speak to whoever has absolute control and
    a) confirm your timeframe,
    b) get a guarantee on times and how he is going to handle it if the program runs overtime — don't accept laughter as an answer.
17. Avoid getting on too late when everybody is tired and they're looking to wind down.
18. Be careful if you are on after coffee and toilet breaks because you will find that the audience is already starting to switch off.
19. Don't ever say that you're tired, sick, nervous, unprepared or upset.
20. Make sure the organizers understand and

accept your complete requirements *before* you leave home. Have your air tickets in advance and the hotel arrangements confirmed and in the organizer's name (if you don't you may receive the bill). Also come to an understanding on the sale of books, tapes and videos.

21. Do not stay in private homes where you are expected to pat the dogs and bounce children on your knees and never have a moment to yourself to relax.

22. Only deal with one person. Do not deal with two or three people if you are going to accept a speaking appointment. It creates confusion.

23. Always check the dress and atmosphere and make sure you fit in.

24. If it is a paid appointment get your deposit on acceptance and your fee and all the money when you arrive — it's rarely sent on time afterwards.

25. Crowds are not a miracle, but a lot of hard work. Do not expect a crowd to turn up this time because you had a big crowd last time. Someone has to get behind the scenes and work up a crowd — it does not happen automatically.

26. Sleep, toilet, eat and exercise at every opportunity. You never know when you may have to keep going without a break.

27. Don't make any firm commitments until you get home (whilst you are in the exciting atmosphere of a speaking appointment, bad judgement prevails).
28. Be very selective in giving free performances because the lack of financial commitment expresses itself in poor preparation, poor programming, poor accommodation, poor attendance and poor results.
29. Do not speak to drunkards — you will never win.

The Best Public Speakers

1. Actors.
2. Professional speakers.
3. Sales demonstrators.
4. Royalty.
5. Masters of Ceremony.
6. Preachers.
7. Business lecturers and teachers.
8. Stewards on airplanes.
9. Politicians.
10. Announcers at airports, bus and railway stations.

Hints for Those Preparing for a Public Meeting

1. Remember crowds are a lot of hard work — send out and follow up 15 to 30 times more invitations than you need people.
2. Have lists for everything — have a countdown and check off the list regularly.
3. Check out the venue several times.
4. If you require a podium for notes, check that there is one available and it has been put up.
5. Have a protector for the speaker; in other words, someone who is with the speaker at all times to be able to handle any of his or her needs.
6. Rehearse time frames with everybody participating in the event.
7. If you are running behind, chop, chop, chop everything and anything except the speaker's time.
8. Let the speaker know in clear, strong terms exactly what time to finish.

9. Avoid having singers or musicians on with a speaker because
   a) they generally want to speak or explain their item before they perform and they are generally bad at it.
   b) their item always takes longer than they tell you it will.
10. Have stirring music while crowds are assembling, seating and dispersing.
11. Have response cards on seats so that the audience can give you feedback.
12. Sell and collect cash for seats well before the event, to be absolutely sure of an audience.
13. You sell more books, tapes and products to a paying audience than a non-paying audience.
14. Low admission prices to hear any speaker generally guarantees a smaller audience.
15. Remember the people who need the message probably won't turn up.
16. Why not rent a crowd — find a group or an organisation that has a large following and make some arrangements with them to use their people for a crowd.
17. Don't forget to give the speaker a plaque to commemorate the occasion or send a thoughtful thank you note — you may need him or her again.

Speak On with Awesome Power

*To speak a word before a crowd, to shout
    directions sure
To claim a new and vital note just so they'll
    ask for more
To move the people further up the ladder
    we call life
To warn the nations of the world of dark,
    impending strife
That's what we're called to do this day from
    platforms grand and small
So we may touch the lives and hearts
    of mankind one and all
And so we speak with awesome power
    to people everywhere
On radio and concert halls, at colleges and fairs
And then at the close of day in motels quiet, alone
Away from cheers and loud applause we always
    dream of home
The day is done, the people gone, and tomorrow
    brings some more
But we just keep pressing on in answer to the calls*